The 2016 Presidential Election Collection

Cartoons by Ben Garrison

This book is dedicated to my wife Tina, who believed in me and stuck by me when she had many reasons not to. — Ben Garrison

FOREWORD by JEFF GIESEA

I've never met Ben Garrison in person, but I have come to know him and count him as a friend. I continue to be amazed as he inspires thousands.

Like many of us during the Trump campaign, we initially met over Twitter and email. I was an admirer of his cartoons, then a customer of his prints. Eventually we became collaborators and friends. Ben would sometimes pick my brain about cartoon ideas. He'd take a basic idea about the news and bring it to life in a cartoon. It felt like magic. And indeed it was, as he made real our collective hopes and imagination.

My favorite work of Ben's is one I commissioned for the pro-Trump art show in New York organized by Lucian Wintrich. It's a watercolor showing multiple images of Andy Warhol wearing a MAGA hat in pop art style. Ben produced it in his unassuming manner, delivering it a few days after discussing it. It's an amazing work. The art show helped launch Lucian's career — he now works as a White House correspondent — and Ben helped launch the art show.

Even after all of our interactions, I still haven't fully humanized Ben. He exists to me as part man, part avatar — the guy wearing a cowboy hat blowing a cigar. I picture him drawing in the yard of a remote Montana home, wearing jeans and a Pendleton shirt. We are overdue to meet in person.

When historians look back at the 2016 election, they will view it as the time when the Right learned to use art to advance its politics, and when citizens and Internet trolls helped propel a candidate into office through social media. I wouldn't be surprised to see museums curate shows like "Political Art in the Age of Trump." Can you imagine Pepe on display at MOMA as a historical artifact?

It's true though: red MAGA hats, "can't stump the Trump" videos, and Ben Garrison cartoons are icons of the golden era of memes that was the Trump campaign. Do you recall the equivalent from the George W. Bush campaign? I don't. Obama's "Hope" poster was iconic but I don't remember much else. "Yes We Can" faded as soon as it was uttered.

This is why this book is so important. Ben's political cartoons are the first draft of history. They document the hero's journey that was the Trump campaign. We all had our roles to play along that journey, and Ben played his best of all. He turned the campaign into a giant comic book, a morality play between good and evil. He made us feel part of it.

As much as Ben's work was about Trump, his best work may be in villainizing Hillary. It is also his most savage. There's Hillary as Humpty Dumpty from her lies, as a prostitute to Wall Street, or collapsing in front of a podium that says "Stronger Together." There's Trump giving her a prisoner's outfit after the second debate, when he said "because you'd be in jail." Then there's Hillary standing beside John Podesta carrying a Satanic-looking "spirit cooking" emblem.

Another theme of Ben's cartoons is Trump's battle against globalists and the establishment. In one of my favorites, Trump stands alone in front of a tank that says "the Clinton machine," evoking

the famous image of defiance from the Tiananmen Square protests of 1989.

Finally, there's the theme of a triumphant Trump. Trump takes the form of heroic figures like Samson, Superman, and Indiana Jones — the paladin we need to clean to clean up Washington and drain the swamp.

The cover of this book portrays Trump as super-human. We all know he's not super-human, but that's not the point. Ben made him larger than life, something we all helped create and bring forth. Ben's cartoons inspired, mobilized, and made us feel part of something bigger than ourselves.

In the Great Meme Wars of 2016, Ben Garrison deserves the Medal of Honor.

Jeff Giesea
February 10, 2017
Washington, DC

America occasionally needs populist presidents such as Andrew Jackson and Donald Trump in order to clean house and get rid of status quo corruption. It took him two terms, but President Jackson drove out the central bankers. Trump's task may be even more difficult because the deep state has become very powerful and entrenched. Both Jackson and Trump sported unusual hair and bushy eyebrows.

CHAPTER 1:
FORESHADOWING

I remember it vividly. I was getting ready to make my daily commute to the city where I worked for the Seattle Post-Intelligencer. I was employed as an artist there. Not as a political cartoonist, but as someone who created design, information graphics and illustration. On this particular morning I was watching the news when a presidential candidate named Bill Clinton was being interviewed. It was the very first time I had seen or heard of him and I was completely unimpressed. I watched the friendly, smiling Clinton with his big hair ingratiate himself to the female host. "What a phony baloney," I thought to myself. "There's no way this con man will ever be president—people will see right through him."

Boy, was I wrong. Not only was he elected president for two terms, but his wife Hillary was considered to be his co-president. We got two for the price of one. We also got a stream of endless scandals. When they finally left the White House, Hillary claimed they were 'broke.' Maybe that's why she stole antiques that she was later forced to return. I figured it was the last we'd have to endure the Clintons. I was wrong again.

Hillary ran for the US Senate representing the state of New York, thanks to JFK Jr. getting bumped off. She won easily. That's when I knew she wasn't going away and that ultimately she would run for president. She had the backing of the globalists and their candidates had a habit of winning. I loathe Hillary. My hatred of her grew over the years. It would bloom to full flower by 2015 and I saw no candidate capable of defeating her. Yes, I was wrong still yet again.

2016 was going to be a year that brought about much needed change.

Drawn in 2014, I didn't realize at the time that there would be even more scandals chasing Hillary.

A cartoon to kick off 2016: Tina and I are shown reeling in the future aboard the "Internata," at GrrrGraphics.com

3

This was the very first Trump cartoon produced by GrrrGraphics. I came up with the idea and Tina wanted to draw it. It spread like wildfire on sites such as 4chan.com

Here's another cartoon drawn by Tina. I drew the headline for her. I must admit she liked Trump before I did.

6   Brexit foreshadowed Trump's victory. My cartoon went viral and was reprinted in many countries.

BREXIT foreshadowed Trump's victory. Pundits and experts didn't think Great Britain could possibly vote to leave the EU, yet they did vote to leave thanks to the work of people such as Nigel Farage. Likewise, Trump's win in America came as a surprise to pollsters and the mainstream media.

People want to have representation and a voice in their governments and not be seen as mere tax sheep to be shorn by the globalists. My Brexit cartoon went viral and was seen by millions. I translated it into German. It was featured on a popular Italian news show. It gave people permission to question the endless immigration by Muslims who do not assimilate well into western culture. I believe this cartoon helped spark and open up debate about issues that needed to be discussed.

Sure, I was smeared over it, too—*The Guardian* voiced their outrage about the cartoon. Andrew Brown said my cartoons reminded him of Nazi propaganda. I've read similar things written by Internet trolls for years, so his scathing attack only made me chuckle. Trolls do not bother me any more, even when those trolls reside at the mainstream media. In the comment section someone said, "I do not find the cartoon racist at all. It's an accurate description of reality." He was not alone in his opinion. I received hundreds of positive emails as a result of the cartoon. Most of that email came from folks in England.

Brown's column may have been written as a warning to others to reject Brexit or at the very least shut up about the subject, but my cartoon resonated. That's because it spoke the truth. Citizens are now realizing that anyone who questions the globalists can expect to get smeared in return. The globalists can't win the debate, so they always resort to using denigration through their puppets known as the mainstream media. People are now aware of those tactics.

Obama considered nationalism to be 'crude.' He was for globalism and America's destruction.

8

Obama preferred blaming Christians, gun owners, and 'bitter clingers,' rather than criticize radical Islam.

Most Americans expected the presidential race to come down to Jeb Bush and Hillary Clinton. They were clearly the picks of the elite establishment political machine. 'They' would win no matter who won the election. The 'Big Club' as George Carlin called it, always got their way. They always won. Americans would get Jeb or Hillary jammed down their throats whether they liked it or not. Both establishment candidates had gigantic coffers and connections. Nobody could stop them.

Many people—especially young people—had other ideas. They wanted someone genuine who could stand up against the machine. Bernie Sanders spoke out against the rampant corruption of the Wall Street elite and the central bankers. Trump wanted to spring minds of Americans from the prison known as political correctness. The coronation of Hillary or Jeb would not come easy for the globalist cartel this time around.

The Hillary machine: Insert money, and she dispenses favors. Also known as 'pay for play.'

Many Americans are fed up with political correctness, but George Soros makes sure it remains well-funded.

11

Beginning late in 2015, I drew cartoons in a small watercolor pad to illustrate the presidential race. My Patreon supporters got to see these cartoons first. This cartoon illustrates how angry the GOP establishment became at the prospect of of a Trump nomination. They did their best to thwart him at ever turn. They cut off their trunks to spite their faces.

CHAPTER 2
IT BEGINS

At first Trump was ignored. His presidential intentions were considered a publicity stunt. I remember watching Bill Maher's show and his panel dismissed him with waves of hands and disparaging laughter. They claimed he had no chance and could be safely ignored.

Sometime shortly thereafter I heard Trump speak. He talked about building a wall and making smart deals that would benefit America and not other countries. He wanted to bring well-paying jobs back to America. It was apparent he was impervious to political correctness, whereas Jeb was completely immersed in globalism. He spewed the predictable PC slogans. Jeb talked about 'loving' illegal immigrants whereas Trump wanted them deported. That really got my attention. Jeb came from the globalist Bush crime family and was considered to be the front-runner, but he also came across as rather wimpy. Trump came across an alpha male. So I decided to draw the cartoon that illustrated the idea (see right). The cartoon was soon seen on many sites throughout alternative media.

I heard Donald Trump say, "One big problem this country has is being politically correct." When he said that, he got my admiration. It was refreshing. Trump was instrumental in breaking the mind control that is political correctness. It was a phrase first coined by Joseph Stalin during the 1920s. Collectivist PC thinking has been relentlessly pushed by the leftist echo chambers that many of our universities have become.

Of all the candidates, Trump was the most fun to draw. He had a tremendous mane of combed-over hair. He had bushy eyebrows and a tapered nose. He was tall and carried himself with an air of confidence. Like Reagan, he knew all about the media and how to bend it to his will. By contrast, Jeb came across as a beta male while Trump stood out among a spate of bland Republican candidates who looked more like the usual suspects. Been there. Done that.

14

The self-funded Trump owed no favors to the establishment. He made the other candidates look like wallflowers.　15

It was revealed that Hillary routinely used burn bags to destroy personal documents, thus flouting protocol. What a surprise.

Yes, Trump was fun and easy to draw, but Hillary was also fun to draw in a different way. Once a fairly attractive woman, Hillary's face now reflects her years of drinking, money grubbing, and scandals. Her contemptuous eyes are the windows of her soul, if she has one.

It was a snap to draw Jeb Bush, too. His smaller nose and high forhead made things easy. Others, such as Cruz and Rubio required a bit more effort. The most difficult politican for me to draw is Al Gore, for some reason.

Bernie Sanders is also easy to draw. He wears glasses and has thinning, disheveled hair, which makes him fun to pen. His strident way of promoting his socialism also played into to his crackpot scientist look. I saw him as a mad Colonel Sanders who used utopian Marxist rhetoric. Yet unlike Hillary, Bernie still had integrity and that appealed greatly to young people. He is among the few politicians who did not get filthy rich while in Congress. He inspired people far more than Hillary ever could, and yet it didn't matter. The DNC would rig the game for Clinton.

At the end, Bernie would set aside his principles and support the bankers' paid-for gal: Hillary.

Tina drew a cartoon featuring Hillary in her bathroom. That's where she kept her illegal server. When asked if she cleaned it, she replied, "Like with a cloth?" What she really used was special software to bleach her server clean. She also used a hammer on cell phones to destroy evidence.

Free stuff is never free. It comes at a cost. It takes away freedom and replaces it with a bloated, tyrannical government that continually expands.

19

By Christmas in 2015, Jeb was already performing poorly in the polls.

I drew the candidates as superheroes. Jeb didn't rate, so I drew him as "The Incredible Shrinking Jeb." His poll numbers also shrank as his campaign went on. Included but not shown here are Cruz, Rubio and Rand Paul.

21

There were no strong third party candidates this go-round. Normally I would vote for the Libertarian candidate, but Johnson was a disaster. He's more of a left-leaning Libertarian than many of us are used to. Sometimes he came across as a bumbling SJW pretending to be Libertarian. Johnson thinks bakeries should be forced to bake sexually suggestive wedding cakes for gay couples. In a free market, nobody should be forced to buy or sell anything. He's right about legalizing marijuana, but perhaps he smoked too much of it himself. In an interview he revealed he didn't know what "Aleppo" was. In another interview he talked with his tongue out and made a fool of himself. Such behavior almost seemed designed to discredit the Libertarian party. Featured here is another page in my election watercolor book.

When the race began, I was leaning toward voting for Rand Paul. I was disgusted when he supported Romney over his own father back in 2012, but I forgave him for that.

I agree with Rand on many issues.

22

BEN GARRISON

LIBIRDTARIAN

To me, ending the Federal Reserve is the most important issue for America. It's one of the reasons I was inclined to support Rand Paul. Donald Trump expressed interest in auditing the Fed, but we'll have to see if that can ever happen. 23

This one was drawn to mark a new year. The establishment in both parties feared and despised Trump because he was an outsider and not easily controlled. His election will force both parties to change.

CHAPTER 3:
DEBATES AND DEBACLES

The first debate featured Fox's attack dog, Megyn Kelly. She didn't ask Trump questions about policy, but rather she attacked his character. "You've called women you don't like 'fat pigs,' 'dogs,' 'slobs' and 'disgusting animals.'" This is the kind of question that set the tone for future mainstream media attacks. Before he ran for president, the media were fine with Trump. Once he ran for president and became viable, they suddenly began smearing him as a racist and misogynistic bigot. This backfired, however. Many people were more disgusted by Megyn's questions than anything dredged up from Trump's past.

To be sure, Trump said some nasty things that were endlessly repeated by the left in the hopes that he would drop out of the race. What amazed me was just how the Democrats happily gave Bill Clinton a pass. Clinton raped and sexually assaulted women and there is plenty of proof to back it up. Trump made some locker room banter and the left treated him like a criminal.

The Republican debates featured a lot of fun moments including a contentious confrontation between Chris Christie and Senator Rand Paul.

Another fun moment: Rubio kept repeating himself robotically when he came under pressure from Christie.

This grim cartoon features Obama the Undertaker at Scalia's gravesite. The Supreme Court justice died mysteriously.

A NEW LOW IN THE GOP DEBATES:
RUBIO GETS "SCHLONGED"

BEN GARRISON
©GRRRGRAPHICS.COM

The low point in the debates: Rubio mentioned Trump's 'small hands' and claimed it meant Trump was under-endowed in other areas. Unfortunately, Trump rose to the bait and denied it was a problem. Embarrassment ensued.

29

30   Cruz won Iowa, but Trump began to run away and win most of the other primaries and caucuses, while protestors disrupted traffic.

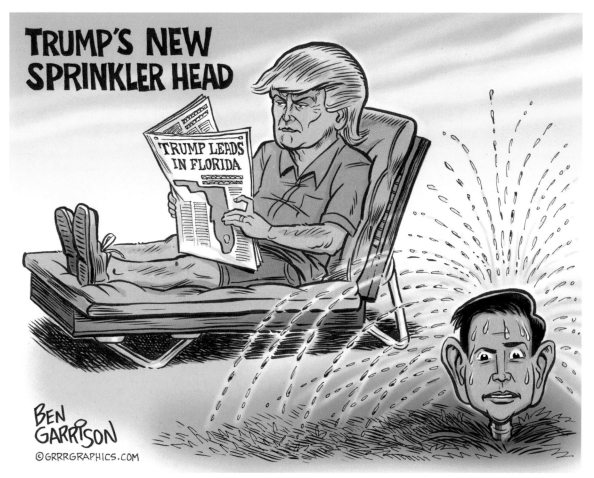

Trump began to 'own' Rubio in the debates. He made fun of Rubio's unfortunate tendency to sweat under pressure.

32   Cruz criticized Trump's "New York Values." The statement backfired on him.

We took some flak from Rubio supporters over the cartoons. I don't hate Rubio. I guess I'm just getting too mean in my old age. Meanness is a quality editorial cartoonists need to have. It was an ingredient I lacked when I was in my 20s. Instead, I was the quintessential 'nice guy,' and a politically correct one at that.

Many years later I read a book by Vox Day titled "SJWs Always Lie." I had never really bothered to learn exactly what a social justice warrior was. Day's book was a real eye-opener. I realized I had been in league with these people in my battle against the trolls. I had also operated under the influence of PC scripts that were drummed into me by schools and the liberal newspapers that I had worked at for many years. I had been operating out of fear. I was afraid of losing work and my reputation. Well, my reputation was sullied and assignments had dwindled. I decided to stop worrying about the trolls and getting called 'racist.' I decided to become who I really was. I had let the cartoons break me. Now they were going to make me.

Today's students are extremely thin-skinned. They are products of constant political correctness drum beating. They have been mollycoddled all of their lives and now they remain engaged in magical thinking, which is at loggerheads with how the world really works. Feelings are of paramount importance to the social justice warriors. They insist that everyone becomes extremely careful and not hurt their fellow hothouse flowers with imaginary slights and micro aggressions. Many comedians will no longer speak at college auditoriums because the kids there can't take a joke.

Forget micro aggressions. My 'Crybully' cartoon was a MACRO-aggression of major proportions. It also got our Facebook page shut down for a period of time. That was a real slap in the face because for nearly five years there were many times when Facebook would refuse to take down pages set up to troll me and ruin my reputation. But insult an SJW? Look out! They will go after you! I received a lot of hate mail. One said he wouldn't rest until I was 'unemployed and living on the streets.' I guess he didn't realize I'm self-employed.

Trump endured constant whining from the legacy media, the GOP establishment BLM, and campus SJWs.

36   Political correctness may lead to dire consequences. Giving into radical Islam could lead to the end of western civilization.

Obama was our first African-American president. He was also our first PC president. Many voted for him to *prove* they weren't racist. Obama was to be the president to end the racial divide.

He also claimed he would be the most transparent administration and be free of lobbyists. His presidency was the most opaque, and it was chalk full of lobbyists.

Obama did his best to achieve completely open borders. He brought in millions of Muslim immigrants. Islam does not integrate well with our Constitution. It's oil and water. The majority of Muslims demand Sharia Law. Their *Quran* tells them to do that. They don't assimilate—they conquer. Obama loves the sound of singing from minarets and was only too happy to bring in as many as possible. Maybe it's what he meant by 'fundamentally changing America.' Hillary wanted to go even further. Using her beloved Merkel as her template, she planned to bring in exponentially more Muslims.

Trump was called the usual names by the mainstream media and the establishment because he wanted to end the immigration by Muslims. He knew that they would import terrorism to our country. He wanted to build a wall on our southern border. Hillary and the globalists wanted no border whatsoever. Hillary told her central banker masters that she wanted an 'open hemisphere.' Who cares about jobs lost and crime suffered by the average citizen? Certainly not the globalist bankers. Hillary detested the average citizen. She identified herself as being part of the team at the very top of the pyramid.

A country without borders isn't a country. Trump's wall became a rallying cry for law and order.

40   Mark Cuban tweeted he'd be happy to debate *any* Trump supporter, but refused Mike Cernovich's challenge.

CHAPTER 4:
HELLACIOUS HILLARY

We had our first black president (half black, actually—his mother was white and his father was probably Frank Marshall Davis) and so the globalist forces thought it was time to get our first female president, Hillary Clinton. She was going to break the so-called 'glass ceiling.' As it happened, she was also the most corrupt, scandal-ridden female politician in history. I decided to do my best to influence a few people and draw her in an extremely negative light. There's no way she should become president. She didn't deserve it by merit, temperament, or accomplishment. She was the most corrupt major candidate in history. Still, many listened to her propaganda arms known as the mainstream media and parroted the obnoxious phrase, "I'm with her." It was supposed to be 'her turn.'

I made it my goal to draw as many anti-Hillary cartoons as I could and I vowed to be just as harsh on her as she had been to her countless victims.

Hillary, like many sociopaths, uses a form of abuse known as 'gas lighting.' The phrase originates from a 1944 film, "Gaslight" starring Ingrid Bergman in which she is tormented by her husband who is trying to make her doubt her own memories. She is made to feel confused and mistaken. She questions her sanity and her ability to remember things correctly.

This is the same tactic Hillary uses. She will lie to our faces and inject ridiculous narratives designed to replace the facts that we know. For example, Russia is to blame for hacking her—forget that this was disproven. She wants us to forget her server was illegal and she and the DNC rigged the primaries against Bernie. The focus moves to boogeyman Russia, whom she complains is backing Trump. Such a lie comes from left field and can be so ridiculous that it's disconcerting. It knocks people off their center as they began to consider such outrageousness. That's gas lighting.

43

Hillary marches recklessly through history. This cartoon was based on an earlier one I drew titled, "March of Tyranny."

During one of the debates Trump told Hillary to her face that he intended to see her prosecuted for her crimes. She responded with a gigantic beaming smile. She's smiling while being threatened with prison? That's a good example of gas lighting. She hoped such a confident smile would suggest Trump's threat as a joke—something from a crazy man. Her smile was saying, "Trump is crazy—you can ignore everything he is saying." To repeat, her smile was a form of gas lighting.

When caught in a lie, she quickly fabricates another. She claimed her "personal email" was *allowed* and used for convenience and it was only on one device. It was later found she had many multiple devices (that she illegally hammered because her yoga emails were private). She said nothing she sent from her illegal server was marked classified. She said 'there is no classified material.' When that was proved to be a lie, she said nothing was marked classified 'at the time.' She said she was aware of what was and what wasn't classified, but then lied and said she didn't know what the "C" in the header meant. Then she said she couldn't remember being instructed about security due to her concussion. Lie after lie designed to confuse and exasperate. Hillary is an expert at gas lighting.

She does such things for fun and sport. Look at her face during the hearings—she enjoys her contemptuous bamboozling of Congress and the American people. It gives her a feeling a power. She doesn't worry about perjury or prosecution. She knows she is above the law.

The cartoon on the right drew many complaints, but to me it sums up Hillary. I drew her as a whore because money and power have always been paramount goals in her life and she will do anythying to anything to obtain both. Many thought I went over the top with this one. Well, too bad. Bernie knew what she was, but he was too politically correct, timid, and polite to denounce her. Maybe he was simply afraid of her. After all, she and her husband have left a large trail of dead bodies behind them over their careers.

THE TWO FACES OF HILLARY

NOT LYING.

LYING.

BEN GARRISON
©GRRRGRAPHICS.COM

Hillary will lie even when the truth may suit her better. She lied about Benghazi being caused by a video. She lied about being named after Sir Edmund Hillary. She lied about her server. She lied about coming under sniper fire.

Hillary is shown here as the 'Queen Bee' stinging America. George Soros is featured on the money that make up her
48 wings. Both cartoons were drawn using Adobe Illustrator, a program that I also use for my commercial art assignments.

I drew this for Groundhog Day. Neither Hillary nor her mainstream media could see her criminal shadow.

49

Broom Hillary: I drew several cartoons showing Hillary as a witch. I was told that it was 'sexist' to portray a woman as a witch. Well, too bad! If anyone deserves to be called a witch, it's Hillary. Trump did indeed ditch her.

Huma cried into the pot when she found out that her husband, Anthony Weiner, had unauthorized email on his laptop. 51

A lot of people sent me ideas based on a "Wizard of Oz" theme. When I penned this, Hillary was having vision problems that caused her eyes to wander. Assange is blowing his WikiLeaks whistle on Hillary. Kaine is the flying monkey.

52

53

A common complaint is I put way too many labels on my work. That's actually an old American tradition. Look at cartoons done over a hundred years ago and you'll find that they're peppered with words. Herblock was famous for having labels all over his work at *The Washington Post*. It was a running joke among the staff there and they would often say, "Have you read Herblock today?" The cartoon on the left page has plenty of labels. I wouldn't have it any other way.

A cartoon without labels is more of an illustration. Some consider editorial cartooning to be the lowest form of political communication. Whoever said that was probably a stuffy editorial page writer. They know people will always read the cartoon first.

An anonymous artist designed a poster featuring the Deplorables. Plenty of memes were created during the election campaign and I was named one of Hillary's 'Deplorables.' I'm proud of that. Hillary made a big mistake and smeared Pepé the Frog as a Nazi and part of Trump's campaign. It was a lie. Unlike Trump, Hillary failed to grasp the importance of memes and it backfired on her.

55

56   Hillary's 'boogiemen:' She tried to link Trump to so called 'right wingers' and Russia. A moonlit Trump 'T' appears on her bed.

Hillary was too old to understand the Internet. She still thought everyone was going to her propaganda arm, CNN for the penultimate, final word in truth. Instead, young people are realizing more and more that the MSM are lying to them. They find the truth tellers on the Internet in the form of alternative media. Hillary found this to be deplorable and used the word 'Deplorables' to describe Trump's supporters in the alternative media. As it turned out, many Trump voters were proud to be called Deplorables and turned it into a meme in and of itself.

Hillary went on a talk show to prove she was healthy by opening a pre-opened pickle jar (there was no popping sound). She also claimed Pepé the Frog, a popular cartoon character used to express a wide range of emotions and issues, was a symbol of hate. Out of hundreds of benign instances, someone added a Nazi armband on Pepé's arm. To Hillary's thinking, it meant Pepé was a Nazi. End of story. She self-righteously announced it on her site and associated the cartoon with Trump. To her, a cartoon frog *proved* Trump was a white supremacist hater. Trump's son used Pepé in a funny tweet. That's why she attacked Pepé. Hillary saw an opening where she could paint Trump as a 'Nazi.'

There's no way she should get to decide such things, but apparently Hillary is the self-appointed Commissar of Hate Speech. She gets to tell us what's what, and the ADL immediately backed her up. "It's official *because we said so*!" Pepé was then vilified in newspapers all over America and Europe as a shocking example of growing hatred. It didn't seem to matter that it was all utter nonsense. It would be more laughable if it weren't so serious. People can now lose their jobs if they post Pepé .

Hillary's ridiculous pronouncements were quickly taught in colleges and the SJWs ran with it. We had using a service to sell coffee mugs with the Pepé image on it. After Hillary decided it was hateful, that service instantly banned our ability to sell the mug.

One professor had an entire class on hateful memes including Pepé. He even included a Pepé cartoon that I had drawn. Only he showed a version that had been altered by trolls. Instead of the slogan "Welcome to Montana," it read "Race War Now," with Pepé stepping on a dead black man. The leftist professor could have easily discovered that it was troll material.

The Pepé incident isn't an isolated occurrence. Jeffery Goldberg, an award-winning reporter and editor at *The Atlantic,* posted a vandalized cartoon on *The Atlantic* blog with my name on it. My cartoon was altered into crude anti-Semitism and he was using it as *proof* of how he was getting harassed by haters and Trump supporters from the 'far right.' Only his cartoon example *wasn't legit*. He finally and grudgingly added a reference to it being the work of trolls after I loudly complained. The media too often repeats lies to fit a narrative.

Soon after she declared a cartoon frog to be a 'symbol of hate,' Hillary began having persistent coughing fits. Was it the curse of Pepé and 'Kek?' (Kek is 4chan's god of laughter). Hillary's health was an obvious and alarming factor in her defeat. Her epileptic fits, uncontrollable wandering eye movements, blue glasses, and out right fainting spells could not be hidden by her campaign operatives. I began drawing more cartoons about her poor health (see next chapter).

A cartoon based on Robert Crumb's "Keep on Trucking" meme. "Cankles" refers to Hillary's wide ankles.

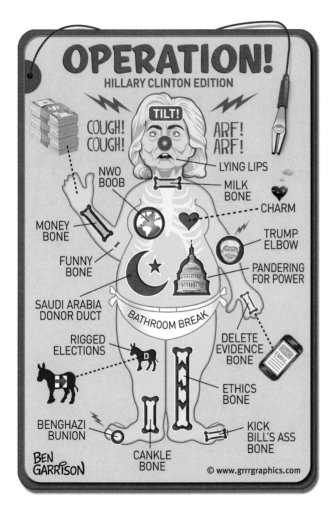

CHAPTER 5:
HILLARY CLINTON HAS A GREAT FALL

Cough cough cough!

That's how it began. Hillary couldn't stop coughing. At first it was blamed on allergies. She said she was 'allergic to Trump.' Then it was blamed on pneumonia. Whatever it was, it was obvious Hillary had serious health problems that went beyond a respiratory illness. She was falling a lot. In 2012, she fainted and struck her head. She received a concussion and many questioned whether or not her brain damage had fully healed.

Video footage showed her having a seizure. Her head bobbled uncontrollably. She had to wear special blue glasses to prevent the seizures. She had a doctor at her side ready to administer medication. She had trouble controlling her eyes. She even barked like a dog. I concluded Hillary was unfit to be president. What if she got the call at 3 a.m. and was 'out of it?' What if she was under the spell of one of her famous violent fits? She has a reputation for throwing things while loudly cursing. Such a person should not have access to the nuclear button.

61

WEEKEND AT HILLARY'S

I DON'T FEEL NO WAYS TIRED

CNN

STRONGER TOGETHER

BEN GARRISON
©GRRRGRAPHICS.com

64   What Hillary might have looked like had she become president. It was also made into an animated .gif file by an anonymous artist.

Low-energy Hillary needed a special stool because she could not stand for long periods of time.

At a 9-11 memorial event, Hillary again fell ill. She had to be escorted to a special medical van and she was unceremoniously tossed into it as if she were a sack of potatoes. Her handlers did not seem concerned or surprised. Hillary's collapses had apparently become old hat. They were expected. On this occasion, one of her shoes fell off and it was left behind. I began adding the shoe to many of my cartoons. It stood for her lack of control over her health. She was unfit to be president physically and morally. Her track record in politics was one of failure. The shoe symbolized this failure. I began featuring her as half shoeless in many cartoons. My followers began looking for her missing shoe. I was surprised that this device tickled so many.

Her so-called husband Bill also appeared to have health problems. He was caught nodding off during her acceptance speech. He looked gaunt and wrinkled. He reminded me of the painting in "Dorian Gray." The debauchery showed on his face. Perhaps it was due to his profligate lifestyle, which included many cocaine binges. By comparison, Trump appeared to be robust and tireless. During the debates it was necessary to make Hillary appear taller, but Trump still loomed over Hillary both in terms of physical and intellectual presence.

The bought and paid for moderators were clearly on Hillary's side. In fact, she received questions in advance so she could spurt out well-rehearsed, carefully planned answers. Hillary was never comfortable speaking to crowds. She came across as forced and fake. She preferred speaking to her Wall Street banker buddies and insiders. She had contempt for the average citizen. She came off as entitled and as if the election should be hers by default and without too much effort or bother. She summed up her attitude when she questioned why she wasn't already up by "50 points." It was difficult for her to keep her arrogance in check.

I quickly drew cartoons after each debate. In each, Trump had to deal with pro-Hillary moderators.

67

STAR TREK 50TH ANNIVERSARY!

A commemorative cartoon by BEN GARRISON

Time to make America great again, Mr. Pence. Ahead, warp factor 7!

CAPTAIN TRUMP

She receives instructions from the Romulans through her ear piece...

COUGH! COUGH!

=HACK=

YES LIE NO

With apologies to Capt. Christopher Pike

CAPTAIN HILLARY

VS.

I drew this for the *Star Trek* original series anniversary. Hillary is shown to be Captain Pike. In the original series episode, "The Menagerie," a tragically injured Pike is kept alive by a life support console. Pike's communication is limited to two lights that signal yes or no. I added a 'lie' light for Hillary. She uses that one the most.

"THE DEBATE SOUVENIR"

After a slow start in the debates, Trump began to dominate Clinton.

By the third debate, Trump came out swinging and was the decisive winner. CNN said Hillary won.

71

CHAPTER 6:
A TALE OF TWO NOMINEES

Trump did a good job hammering Hillary's corruption during the debates. Loretta Lynch, the Attorney General, also became complicit when Bill Clinton boarded her plane to make some sort of deal or threat (which is in and of itself a crime).

Obama was also involved. He had long known about Hillary's illegal server. A 'sorry' from Hillary about that matter isn't enough. She has a long history of pushing the envelope on purpose. She must derive some sort of sick thrill from playing Americans for fools. Cattlegate, Filegate, Travelgate, Benghazi, Whitewater, Vince Foster, Haiti and the pay-for-play Clinton Foundation are just some of her other devious capers.

Hillary outright stole many primaries and the nomination from Bernie. *It was all rigged*. WikiLeaks made that crystal clear. Debbie Wasserman Schultz took the fall for Hillary. After she lost the election, Hillary the rigger used her Alinsky-inspired projection method to blame Trump for rigging things. She claimed Trump had the help of so-called 'Russian allies.' That's right—Hillary dredged up McCarthyism as a weapon to be used against Trump. She seemed to be doing her best to bring back the Cold War. She also resorted to her old tactic of blaming her long list of wrongdoings on a 'vast right wing conspiracy.' Hillary and her historic vagina were never subject to the laws of the land. She considered herself above the law. She was the most qualified candidate *ever*. CNN said so, so it must be true, right?

What did Bernie do after he found out that Hillary rigged the game and had stolen it from him? He endorsed her, of course! Bernie Sanders lost all credibility after that. Hillary represented the status quo, Wall Street central bankers and war. She was the very face of the corrupt, top one percent establishment. If Bernie had loudly condemned Hillary for her corruption, he would have been hailed as a hero. Instead he promised his groveling support. It was one of the biggest back stabs in political history.

"RUBBING HIS NOSE IN IT"

Hillary may have blackmailed or threatened Bernie in some manner to force him to go along.

Bernie torched his ardent supporters when he announced he was 'with her.'

This is a commissioned cartoon for Stefan Molyneux, who very eloquently argued against Hillary Clinton.

The Trump Train gained steady momentum. A tireless campaigner, he gave robust speeches to overflow crowds.

Hillary tried her best during the debates to get Trump to 'go for the bait.' Often she succeeded, so I drew a cartoon that urged Trump *not* to rise to her taunts. As it turned out, Hillary had all the debate questions given to her in advance. She loved a rigged game. Hillary and her DNC also rigged primaries against Bernie Sanders — especially in California.

An alpha lion, Trump was the star of the GOP circus. The establishment tried in vain to tame him.

80   Trump slam dunked Cruz through the 'basketball ring' in Indiana. Glenn Beck was heartbroken.

Donald Trump was the populist, nationalist candidate that most of the country wanted. People were waking up and they knew that both parties were compromised and controlled by a global elite who usually owned and controlled both nominees. It didn't matter who won as long as they continued to pull the strings. Trump was his own man. He paid for his campaign himself and was beholden to nobody. America had not had such a candidate since perhaps Ronald Reagan. All stops were pulled and all measures used to stop him. Trump was endlessly smeared, ridiculed, and attacked, but his 'Make America Great Again' juggernaut could not be stopped.

81

82

Trump chose Indiana governor Mike Pence for his vice president. He was probably selected to attract votes from the Republican Christian right. An accomplished speaker, he seemed to balance out the Trump's volatile reputation.

83

84   Hillary's 'right hand person,' Kaine, did little to help Hillary. His PC persona could not muster much enthusiasm.

WikiLeaks revealed the scam known as Hillary Clinton, but Bernie ended up taking the rigging against him meekly.

85

86   Obama was supposed to end racial division. Instead, he widened the divide. He was the race baiter in chief.

The mainstream media continued their relentless and shameless drumbeating for Hillary. They claimed the polls showed she was well ahead in the race, but the louder they cheered for Hillary the more people went elsewhere to find the truth. They found it on the Internet and the alternative media. Drudge, Alex Jones, Mike Savage, Zero Hedge, Jeff Rense, and many others such as Mike Cernovich, Paul Joseph Watson, David Seaman, and Stefan Molyneux, were the voices of reason. Even those on the progressive left such as H.A. Goodman spoke out strongly against Hillary.

The party conventions were a good illustration of blue states vs. red states. It also exposed just how weak Hillary was. She had to *pay* for people to show up and cheer for her while also turning on noise machines to drown out protestors, who ended up walking out. The Republican Convention exhibited far more enthusiasm despite Cruz's refusal to endorse Trump. Cruz was loudly booed. Chants of 'lock her up' were heard repeatedly much to the abhorrence of the mainstream media who continued to paint Trump as a monster. Hillary and George Soros were determined to stir up trouble and violence against Trump, and one of the tactics they used was racial division.

Hillary made her acceptance speech dressed in angelic white. "Stronger Together" was her campaign slogan, but as her campaign went on it would have been more appropriate for it to be 'Stranger Together.' Her allies ignored her criminal deeds and scandals and insisted that unlikeable Hillary was the overwhelming favorite. They ignored the working class and took African Americans for granted. All she had to do was speak in politically correct platitudes. Many thought she had it in the bag.

Earlier I drew a cartoon showing Hillary kissing the ring of the Devil just before making her convention acceptance speech. It turned out to be a prophetic cartoon.

What WikiLeaks revealed was something right out of "Eyes Wide Shut." Americans have had their eyes shut for far too long. John Podesta's emails revealed rituals so disgusting that I will not repeat them here. Many said there was plenty to suggest he was also associated with pedophile rings.

These people are *evil*. They engage in satanic practices in order to gain dominance. They want power over the populace and they have succeeded. It's now time to expose these monsters. Both Hillary and Bill made many trips to Jeffrey Epstein's 'Pedophile Island.'

It should be no surprised that the Clintons have put vast sums of money into banks in the Middle East. They have their escape hatches ready.

90   While Americans were occupied with the Christmas holidays, Obama began handing over their Internet to global control.

Meanwhile, Obama began handing over the Internet to the UN. It may have only have been the Internet 'address book,' and many say nobody will even notice the change—but it's only the first step. If this weren't important, Obama wouldn't be giving it away.

Globalist traitors such as Obama do things in increments. That's how they slowly boil the citizen frogs—unless it's a meme frog such as Pepé. They tossed him into the rolling hot water right away. As soon as he was listed on the ADL as offensive, newspaper articles around the world began publishing pages explaining how dangerous he is. It's both outrageous and ridiculous, but it's also ominous. This is how free speech dies.

The globalists also want to create their own memes. They began calling real journalism on the Internet 'fake news.'

The Internet has flourished under US control. Aided by our First Amendment, the Internet has enabled us to find truth to counter the incessant propaganda narratives being spewed by the completely non-objective mainstream media. The US developed the Internet. We paid for it. Why give it away? It is being given away because the globalists want a Chinese-style approach, which will enable them to contain and control free speech on the Internet.

As the election date neared, I drew as many cartoons as I could in the hope that I could sway a few minds and help the undecided voters decide for Trump. One of the sayings Trump had come up with was, 'drain the swamp!' It was a natural for a cartoon. It went viral and I sold the original drawing within hours. I was shocked and amazed! We also sold a great many autographed prints and I wrote on them, "Pull the Plug!"

DRAIN THE SWAMP!

Someone suggested I draw Trump as a bomber pilot. I added a scene from *The Twilight Zone* for extra humor.

94   This cartoon is based on the famous Tiananmen Square photo taken by Jeff Widener of *The Associated Press.*

I drew a final cartoon on election eve and released
it the next morning along with this short essay:

Donald Trump is a builder. He makes progress. He accomplishes positive things. He
wants to bring good into the world. He took a million and a half dollar inheritance and
turned it into many billions. Now he wants to do the same for America.

Is he a perfect human being? No one is. But there's something to be said for a man who
just spent over a year of his life doing something for his country when he could have
retired in comfort.

As for Hillary, she's a scandal-ridden criminal. She should be in prison. Right now.
Instead, she has a chance of becoming president. This must not happen. She puts herself
and her cronies first.

Do the right thing, America. Vote for someone who places America first. Vote for Trump.

—Ben Garrison

IT'S YOUR CHOICE, AMERICA!

CHAPTER 7:
AFTERMATH

It was a tense evening at first. The mainstream media expected an easy Hillary victory and they already seemed to be celebrating. I had repeatedly predicted a Trump landslide, but I was worried Hillary would somehow rig the vote in her favor. As the evening wore on, it was clear that Trump would win. It seemed like it would take forever to receive the final score, though.

Podesta came out to speak for Hillary. He told her devoted followers to 'go home.' I thought it was disgraceful that Hillary couldn't speak to her supporters herself. Apparently she had succumbed to another violent, drunken rage and she actually tried to physically assault some of her staff. It is said she smashed a ridiculously expensive bottle of champagne into an equally ridiculously large and expensive 4K TV set that Saudis had given her. She threw a heavy figurine that had been atop a celebratory victory cake across the room and it lodged in the drywall. It is said sedatives were added to her drink. She was in no condition to speak to her supporters. She was unfit to be president.

Trump won and made an energetic acceptance speech at around 3 a.m. I had already turned in, but Tina woke me up so we could watch his speech together. It was over. He had put in a superhuman effort against all odds and he won.

A SUPERHUMAN EFFORT

BAGS of SORROWS

Trump was elected president of a country with a government that is no longer responsible to 'We The People.' Globalist central bankers and the deep state rule us. George Soros and other oligarchs pull the strings. They no longer care if we know. It's 'in our face.' They want America broken down and remolded to their liking. Hillary was supposed to have finished where Obama left off. She was to do their bidding. Her corruption is grandiose in scale. It was openly on display. She considered herself 'above the law' because she has been protected by powerful figures. Americans soundly rejected this situation by electing Trump.

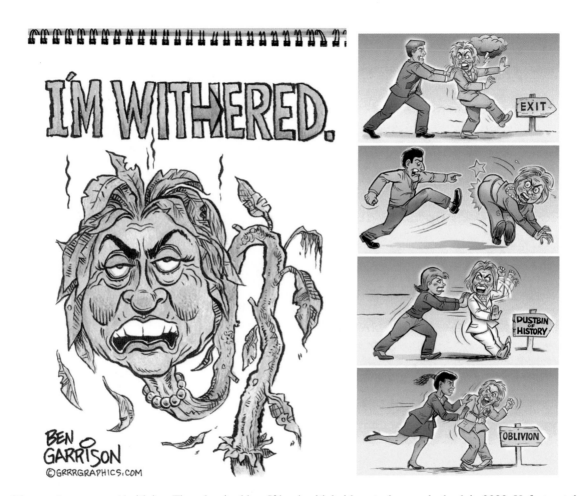

Many voters were not 'with her. They despised her. If her health holds out, she may be back in 2020. Unfortunately.

Boo hoo! Many celebrities cried up a storm while President Elect Trump was singing in the rain.

As Trump supporters celebrated, many on the left were crying crocodile tears. They were both incredulous and inconsolable.

CNN reported Aaron Sorkin's letter of comfort to his daughter. Sorkin reassured her that he would stand up to the dangerous President Trump and not move to Canada like so many other celebrities had threatened to do if Trump won. Those celebs have since reneged on their promise. (Besides, Canada doesn't want them).

In his fear-filled screed, Sorkin said this:

"…it wasn't just Trump who won but the Ku Klux Klan, white nationalists, sexists, racists and buffoons."

How delusional is this man to think that millions of Trump voters are somehow members of the Klan? Is he smearing roughly half of America as 'racist' simply because they see the folly of open borders and unaffordable health care? Are they racist because they want to end the rampant corruption and see jobs brought back to our country? 'America first' used to be patriotic. Now one is called racist or a 'buffoon' simply for being against collectivism.

Mr. Sorkin exemplifies the celebrity crybabies and protestors who are now dancing tantrums over Trump's victory. They are out of touch with reality and evidence. Apparently the propaganda arms known as the mainstream media were successful in brainwashing many. The globalist billionaire Soros also has a lot to do with funding the protests and conflict in America.

The resistance toward Trump removed all doubt about who's really running the show. It's not us. It's not the American people. It's the globalist entity. The shadow government. The dark state. Those snakes have now been driven out of their holes because of their obvious and frantic effort to get Hillary elected. Patriots who were once reviled as being 'conspiracy nuts' have now been proven to be right. They are now no longer conspiracy 'theories.' They're REAL conspiracies, and they're being conducted by criminals.

Hillary accepted millons of dollars in donations from Saudi Arabia, a country that won't allow women to drive.

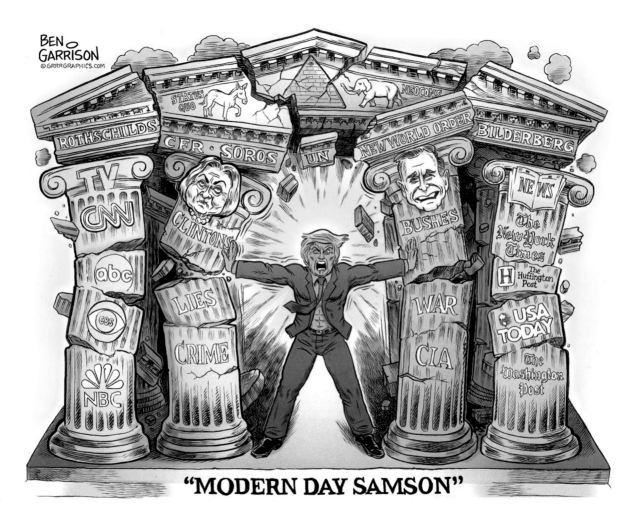

"MODERN DAY SAMSON"

CNN continued their Trump trash talking even after he was elected. President elect Trump had a meeting with media heads at Trump Tower and let them all have it. He told Wolf Blitzer, "CNN is a liar and you should be ashamed!"

Too many in the GOP fought hard to stop Trump. I didn't want to see them invited to the president's victory party.

Trump did meet with Romney (who previously railed against him), but he did not bite the 'Apple of Compromise.'

107

They say it's not over until the fat lady sings, but Hillary kept on singing, She wanted recounts and then even suggested the election had been 'hacked' by the Russians, who she claimed were in league with President Trump.

President Trump may be our last, best hope to tip the balance away from the globalist shadow government.

110

To truly make America great again, we must end the Federal Reserve and its immoral system of debt currency.

111

The dangerous lame duck Obama threatened Russia over their alleged 'hacking of the election.'

115

116   The hot-headed Senator John McCain suggested the western world was uniquely imperiled by President Trump.

The far left and shadow government engaged in a lot of swearing and gnashing of teeth just before the inauguration.

118   This cartoon was inspired by Trump's inauguration speech.

Trump predicted a Patriots' victory. They made the most improbable comeback in Super Bowl history.

119

120   Jerry Brown (Gov. "Moonbeam") as the California cat lady. Trump stands against this kind of open border socialism.

Just when people thought Hillary was off the stage for good, she's making rumblings about another presidential run. The globalist meddler and Hillary supporter George Soros is doing his best to destroy the Trump administration. Obama is also anxious to protect his legacy by thwarting Trump.

Hillary is a lying hypocrite who couldn't accept defeat. She also couldn't accept blame. She and Obama are blaming the Russians and Trump's supposed involvement in their 'hacking' of the election. Obama's activities border on sedition. It's time for the Clintons and Obama to finally step off the world stage, but they never seem to go away. Who knows—maybe Michael...er...Michelle Obama will end up running for president. Chelsea Clinton, too. There will be endless possibilities for more cartoons.

I designed and illustrated a silver coin that commemorates President Trump.

CHAPTER 8:
AFTERSHOCKS

It became clear that Hillary, Obama, and Soros were NOT going to accept a Trump presidency without a push back. Soros funded protests and marches. After a vacation in Palm Springs and the Caribbean, Obama moved to a mansion in DC and began plotting Trump's takedown. He has the help of his former advisor, Valerie Jarrett. They are now plotting to thwart President Donald Trump. This amounts to sedition.

Hillary got a new hairdo and began making very odd videos in which she urged women to 'resist.' Resist what? Aren't women already equal under the law? She also dropped hints about running for the mayor of New York, but my guess is that she'll simply hang around for the next four years and try to remain relevant before running for president a third time—despite her unpopularity. Will the old lady's health hold out for another run?

Who else do the Democrats have? Elizabeth Warren, who once claimed she was part Indian? Creepy touchy-feely uncle Joe Biden? They may as well resurrect Anthony Weiner. What about getting Michelle Obama to run? Regardless, it appears the glass ceiling for a female president will remain intact for a while longer.

This is all a small matter compared to the latest WikiLeaks revelations. "Vault 7" confirmed that Americans no longer have a Fourth Amendment. It has been completely trampled. We can no longer expect any privacy. The Deep State consists of entities such as the FBI, the CIA, and the NSA. They spy on us and store all data in large complexes. Our politicians are blackmailed. Citizens can be assassinated and the CIA can make it appear accidental. This creates an environment of fear and many are afraid to speak out.

WikiLeaks also showed that Trump and his campaign had been heavily wiretapped by Obama. This is an outrage even more egregious than Watergate, yet it remains to be seen if Obama will go to prison. That's where he and the Clintons belong. We now have a cold civil war of sorts. Globalism and tyranny on one side, and on the other side, freedom loving nationalists who want to **Make America Great Again.**

The corporate mainstream media exposed themselves as propaganda shills for the elite status quo.

124 WikiLeaks revealed the CIA knew Obama had wiretapped Trump. Barack belongs in a federal prison.

Mexican politicians were used to US politicians giving into them at every turn. That's not how Trump plays the game.

126   Obama tried to fundamentally change (destroy) America so he could help his masters usher in globalism.

We The People have been replaced by We The Shadow Government. They pull the strings, not the voters.

Le Pen is mightier than the sword

Marine Le Pen may be the Trump of France. She's against the corrupt French establishment and endless Muslim immigration.

Obama remained in Washington D.C. He and George Soros formed a seditious plot to destroy Trump's presidency.

129

CHAPTER 9:
RESOURCES

This book would not have been possible without my supporters. In 2015 I was ready to throw in the towel and stop drawing cartoons altogether. The trolls had caused me plenty of grief and lost work. I've quit on too many things in life though, and so with the help of Tina, I decided to draw even more cartoons. We started a Patreon page, where people could donate to artists, writers and musicians and help them financially. At first we had only a handful of supporters, but it began to snowball during the election year and it has been my honor and privilege to receive more support than I would have ever expected.

Even better, a collector named John M. from Kansas began purchasing a great many of my originals including cartoons drawn years ago. He really helped us more than he can know. I hope he can resell all those cartoons at higher prices some day. I also received donations from many generous individuals. You know who you are and your help is greatly appreciated.

I began doing interviews and podcasts and that brought us more attention and validation. The Internet trolls continue to recede into the distant shadow land where they belong.

I had a tremendous lot of cartoon ideas emailed to me from people all over the world. At one point later in the year I was receiving at least a half dozen ideas per day. This came as a surprise and I regret only being able to draw a handful of those ideas. I always try to add a credit to the contributor. 2016 also brought a huge increase in the email I receive. Sure, I still get hate mail, but the vast majority of the mail sent to me was positive. My only regret is sometimes I just don't have the time to answer all of it.

All of this has been overwhelming and extremely inspiring. Thanks again to all my friends who made 2016 a year to remember. 'Stay tooned' for more cartoons!

LINKS

Our main site:
http://grrrgraphics.com/index.html

Patreon page:
https://www.patreon.com/grrrgraphics

Facebook:
https://www.facebook.com/RealBenGarrisonCartoons

Twitter:
@GrrrGraphics
https://twitter.com/GrrrGraphics

Gab:
https://gab.ai/GrrrGraphics

Instagram:
https://www.instagram.com/grrrgraphics/

Tumblr:
https://www.tumblr.com/blog/grrrgraphics

WP Blog:
https://grrrgraphics.wordpress.com

Fine art:
http://www.bengarrison.com

You Tube:
https://www.youtube.com/user/bgarri57/videos

Buy T-shirts
https://teespring.com/stores/grrrgraphics-t-shirts

eBay
http://www.ebay.com/usr/grrrgraphicscartoons

The author sketches out a cartoon idea in northwest Montana.

131

SPECIAL THANKS TO ALL OF OUR PATREON SUPPORTERS!

Bob P, Evan D, Scott D, Karl W, Paul S, Christopher L, Martin, PAZ, Gus V, Wild Bill, Brandon D, Steve S, Jacob, Daniel F, Sr. Deplorable, Patty W, Paul M, Winston C, Anthony F, Houston C, Haridas T, Napoleon86, Claire H, Alex S, Todd T, Clay H, Brandon C, Del B, Raymond P, Nick, Maxim S, Peter W, Josh C, 8055, David R.W, Sean M, David D, Donna M, Frank L, Joshua M, Ramona V, NinjaStuff, Donald T, Jerry M, Fred H, Bonnie M, Lasse E, Michael M, Sean P, Daniel D, Laura L, Stephen G, Tom M, Brian, Andrew L, Douglas H, Alexander W, Hector M, Jim B, John D, Daniel F, Jason P, Manuel K, Cynthia N, Nick R, Seth M, Patrick O, Richard R, Marie P, Luke R, Lori, Karen G, Kristy N, Limerick, The Eradecator, Steve H, Peter Z, Chris, Areg Y, Mark L, Don P, Debbie D, Sean S, Hanna, Bryan M, Joshua L F, Saven V D, Sioux R, Gary S, Patrick D, No Good, Jiri B, Jeff, Arden B, Nathan C, Emily Y, Jason F, Robert B, Michael D, Christopher K, Carl T, Andy F, Andrew D, G P, Hoan TT, Keith R, Judie S, OGK, Andres R, Anton Janet R, Peter M, Reid F, Tom C, Greg P, Alicia G, Conor D, Eirik E, Vitezslav K, Merid H, Bob R, Alan O, Joel B, [|||||], Yuri R, Martin S, Daniel H, Sean D, Alison, Matt R, Olve, Charles P, Jake L, Joseph F, S A, Rylan R, Rich N, Charlie W, Susan L, David, Claire H, Gena C, Jon H, Zan Z, Sam K, Andrew, Malakaira, GG, Robert H, Enoch C, Adriaan W, Stephan P, Caspar K, Daniel, Bob R, Joshua T, Justin E, Alan L, Brian K, Cindy M, Emmett E, Ryan S, Charles B, Harry P, Jan M, Harry C, Josh N, Rianne, El Muncho, Andrew, Julia P, Rossolo, ShockMaster, VT, Shanna R, Cae, Kyle Y, Mark P, Nick, Alex M, Eli D, Moonshield, Brad W, Byran B, Nicholas T, Steven C, Marcus E, Nicholas P, Beverly N, Asari L, T B, Tiago, Adie W, Henry D, M3, Charles B, Richard, Jared E, Fanshun X, Skyler A, Visith T, Liam B, Anthony L, James T, Baki H, Elliott K, Vive Charlie, J S, David F, Christine L, Matt G, Brian R, Eric J, Garret, Evan R, Craig C, Wyatt E, Larry G, Lonnie F, Lucas W, Thrormurn, Jpowap, Duncan S, Sarah T, Ubiquitous Party, Kris, Adam W, Cullen K, Morgan S, and Jason D. (This list is subject to constant change).

Also, thanks to all who donated via our site—you helped make the cartoons in this book possible.

Ben Garrison is an independent political cartoonist based in northwest Montana. Ben began drawing cartoons in 2009 to protest the central banker bailout, bloated government, and globalism. Ben's cartoons have been seen by millions of people around the world. He and his wife Tina, also a cartoonist, created GrrrGraphics.com to speak out against the slide toward tyranny.

Ben graduated magna cum laude from *Angelo State University* with a BA degree. He studied painting under the late Dr. Otis Lumpkin.

Tina Garrison has a BFA degree from *The Columbus College of Art and Design*. She produced many animations for laser shows. She and Ben have worked hard to make grrrgraphics.com a success.

Made in the USA
Columbia, SC
09 October 2021

46867421R10080